floral inspirations

Flowers are beautiful little things. Something small that can bring joy, and put a smile on someone's face. Unfortunately, flowers do not last forever. A beauty that is short lived, even though we wish they could last forever. Flowers are a reminder to enjoy everything in the moment and to find the joy and beauty in the little things, because some things don't last forever. This coloring book is a way to preserve the beauty of flowers, be in the moment, express yourself, and create your own one of a kind bouquets to enjoy!

Brighten up your walls! Each page can be removed and framed to add some colorful art to your life!

Test out your colors on the trial page in the back of this book to see how your markers or pencils work with this paper! Doodle, shade and color away!

There is also an extra page in the back of this book that can be removed to use as a protective sheet behind the coloring page you are working on, just in case your markers or pens bleed through!

Let the colors flow out on these pages and inspire you to look for the beauty and joy in the little things. Now go, create, color and inspire!

Thank you!

Floral inspirations is a coloring book that has been long in the making. I'd like to dedicate this to everyone that has supported me and my artistic journey. Thank you from the bottom of my heart. I cannot wait to see what amazing creations you make in this coloring book! Share your pages with me on my social medias listed below and use #EKfloralinspirations to see what others are creating too!

Floral Inspirations: A detailed floral adult coloring book

ELIZABETH KARLSON

Copyright © 2017 Elizabeth Karlson

All rights reserved. No part of this publication may be reproduced, distributed or transmitted in any form or any means, including photocopying, or other electrical or mechanical methods without prior written permission from the publisher.

ISBN: 1979746354
ISBN-13: 978-1979746359

Printed by CreateSpace, An Amazon.com Company

Available from Amazon.com, CreateSpace.com, and other retail outlets

www.elizabethkarlson.com
Instagram: @elizabethkarlsonart
Facebook.com/ElizabethKarlsonArt
elizabethkarlsonart@gmail.com

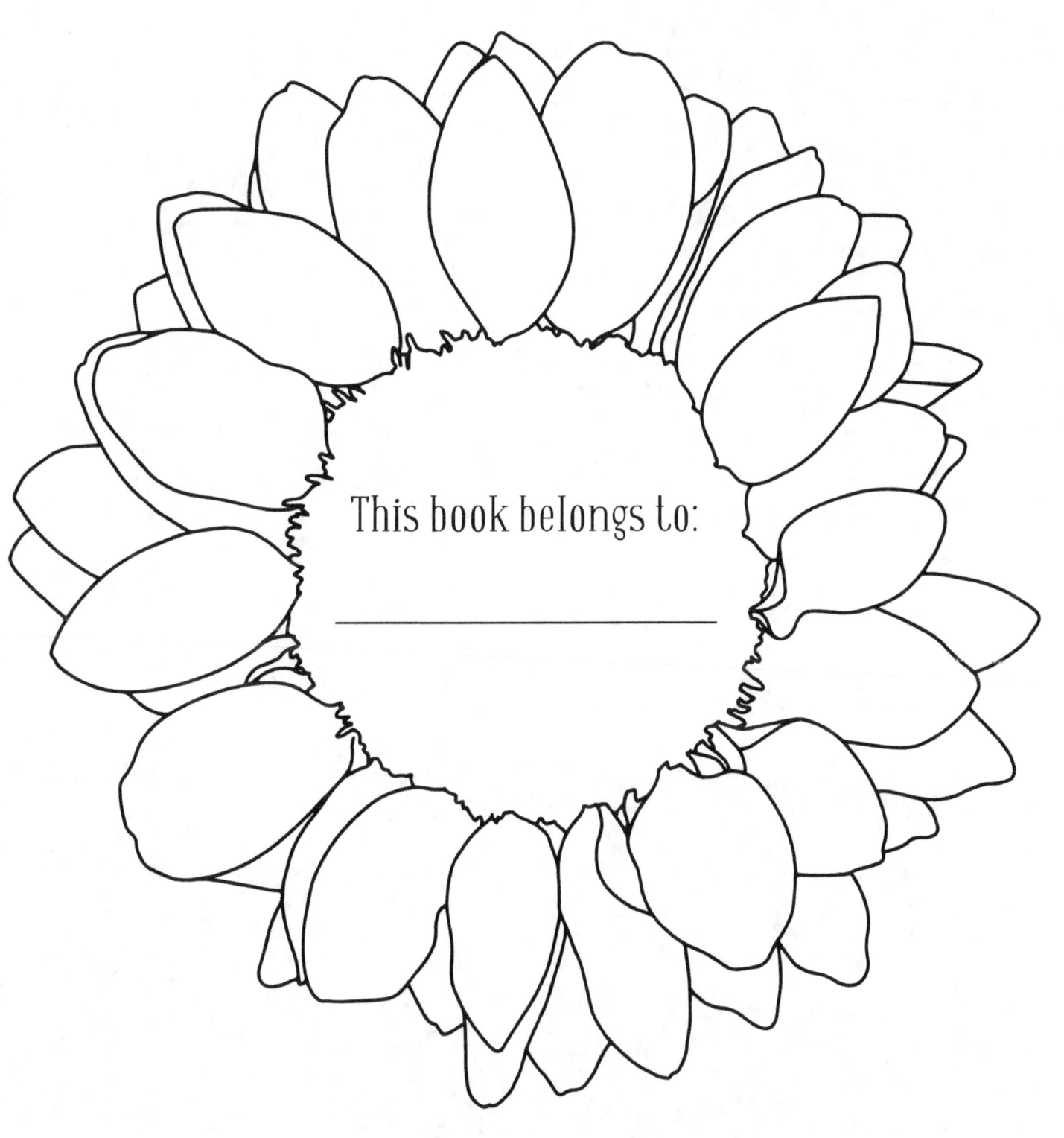

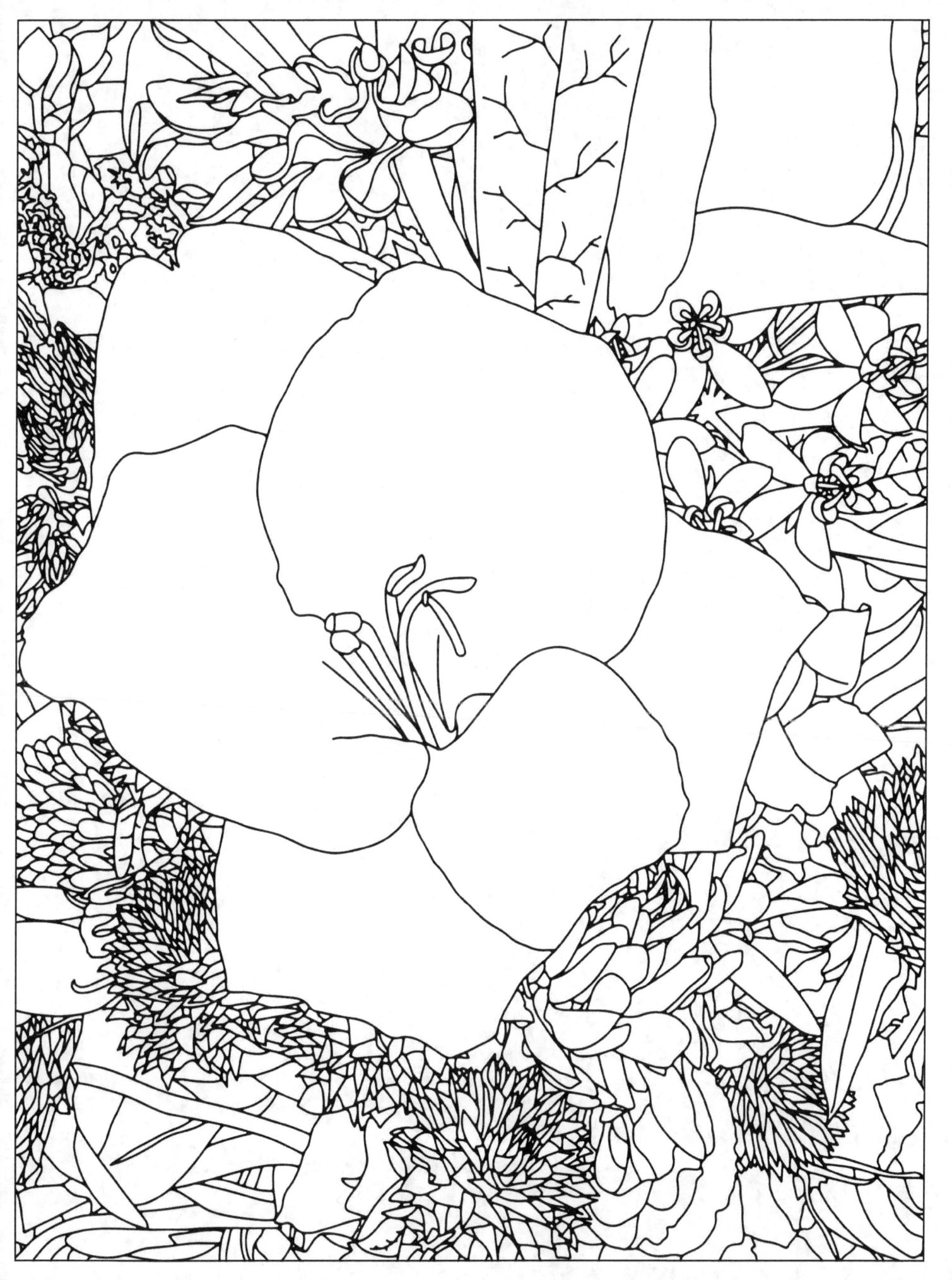

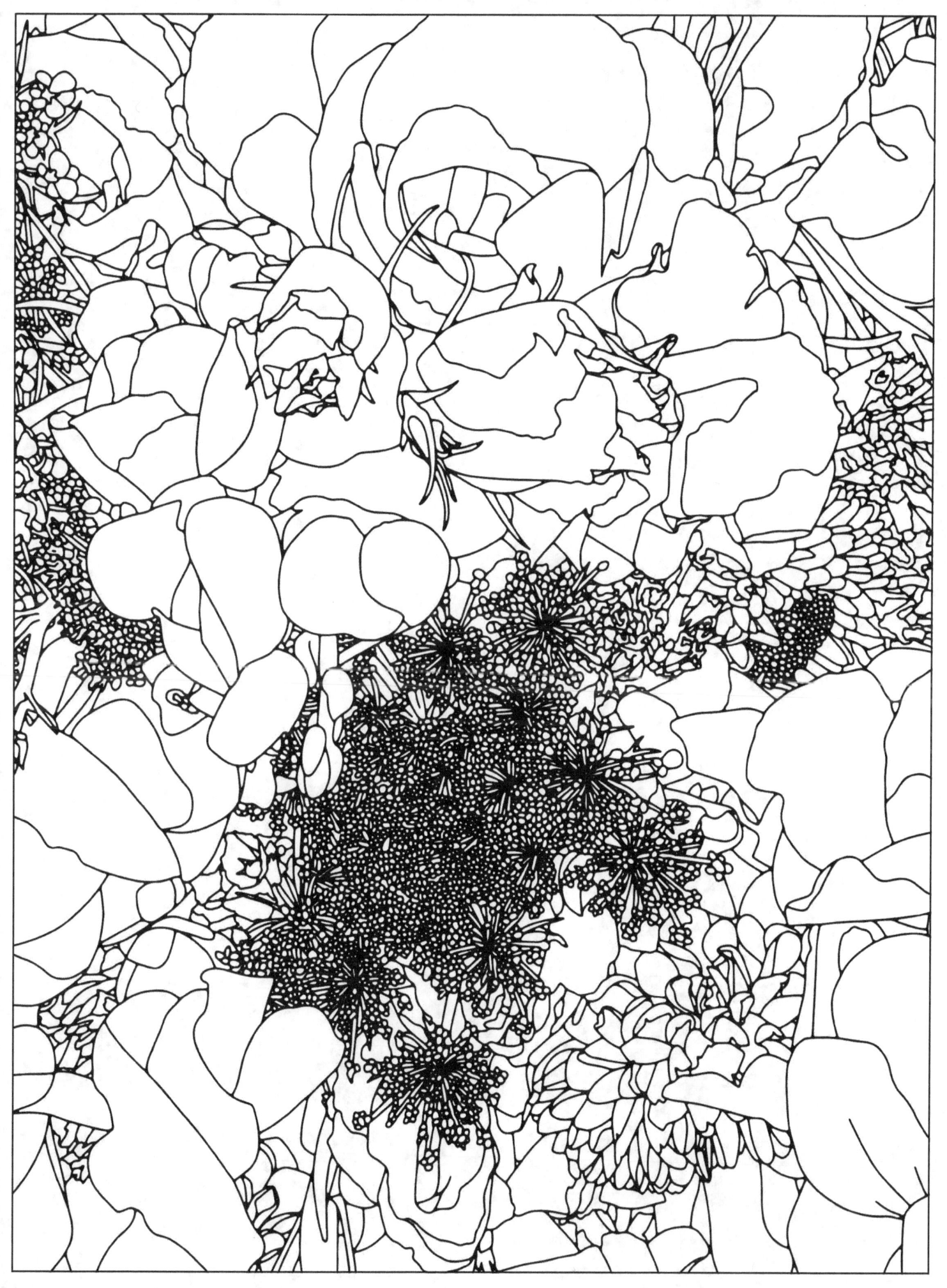

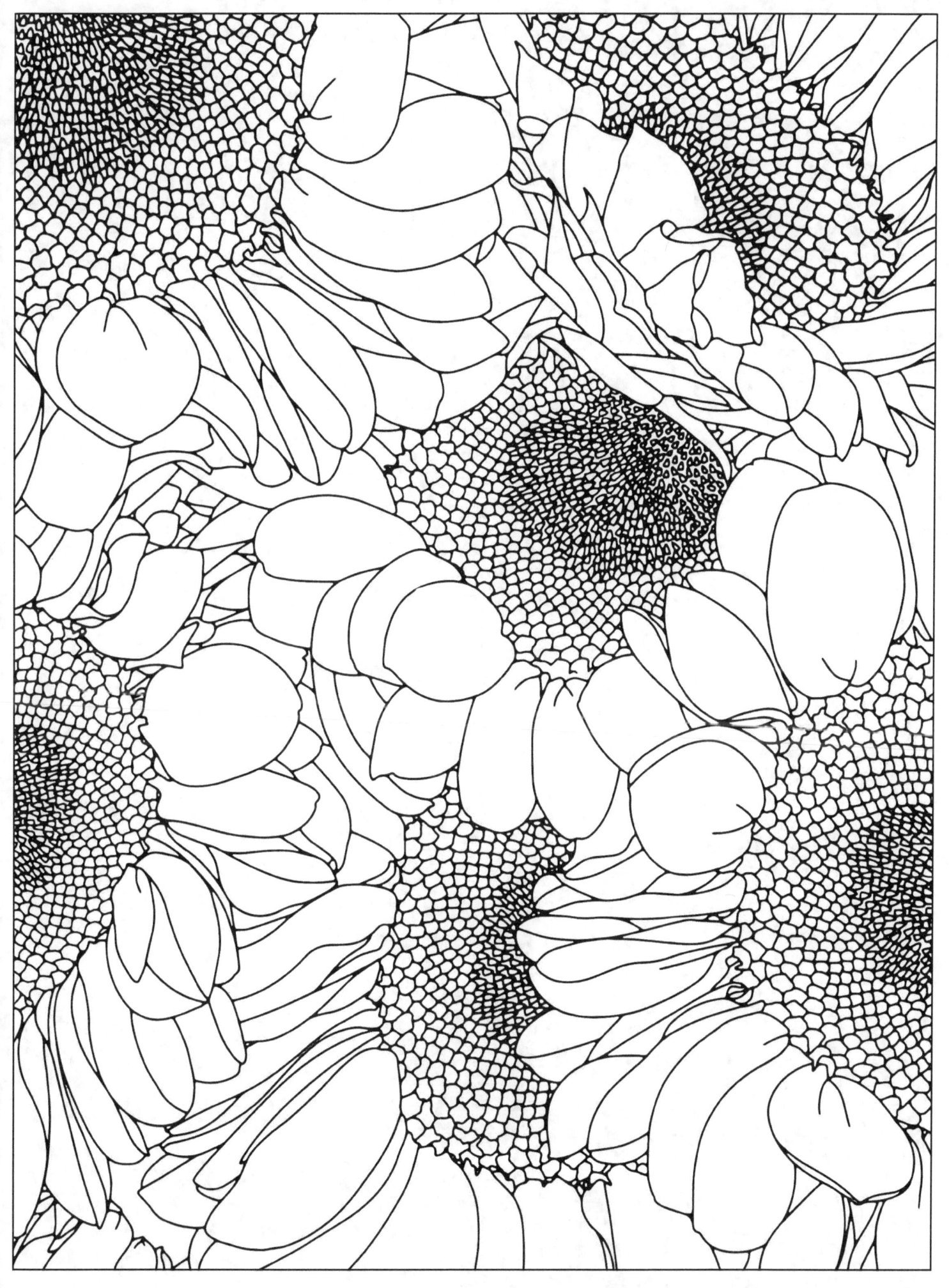

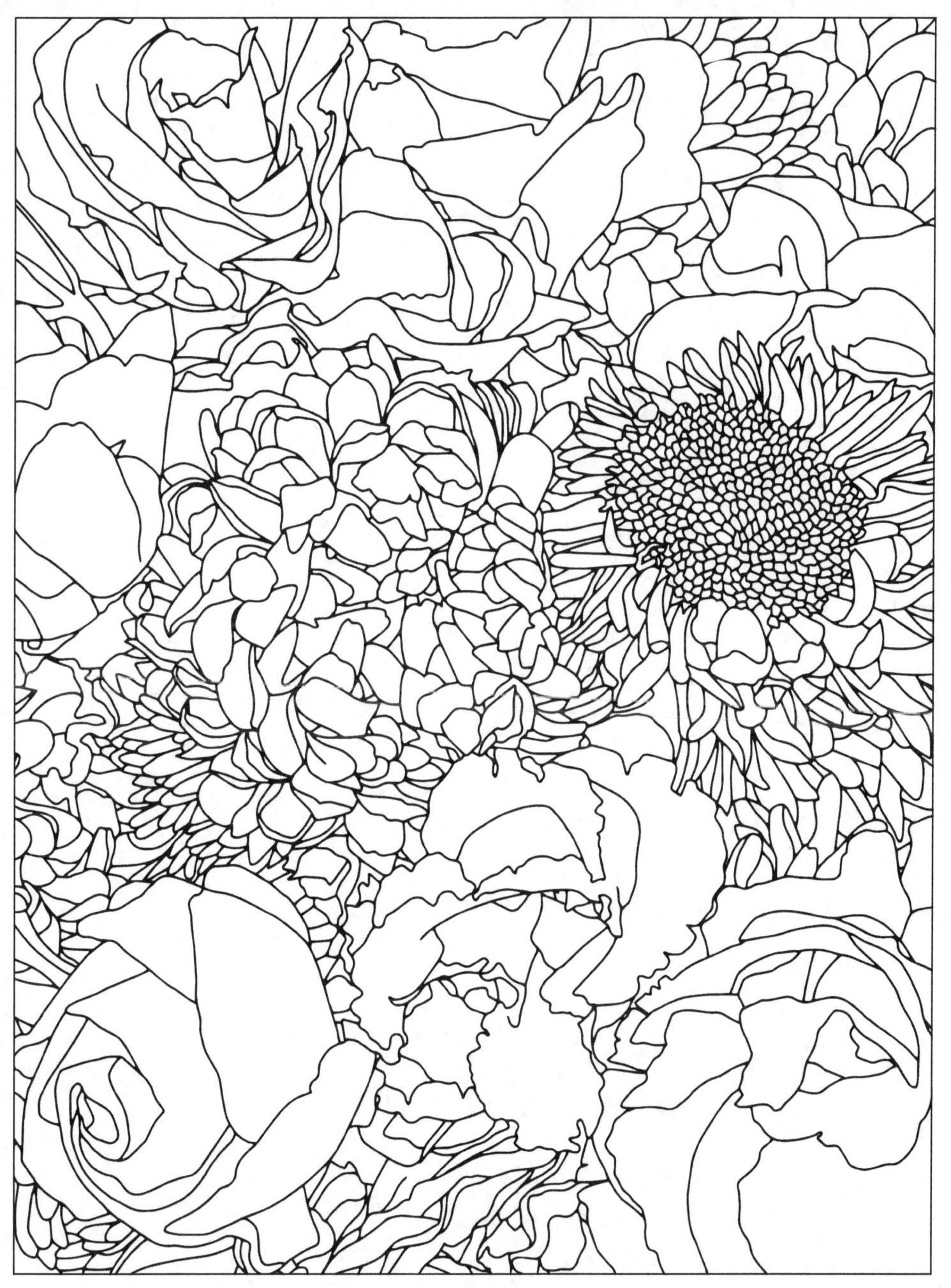

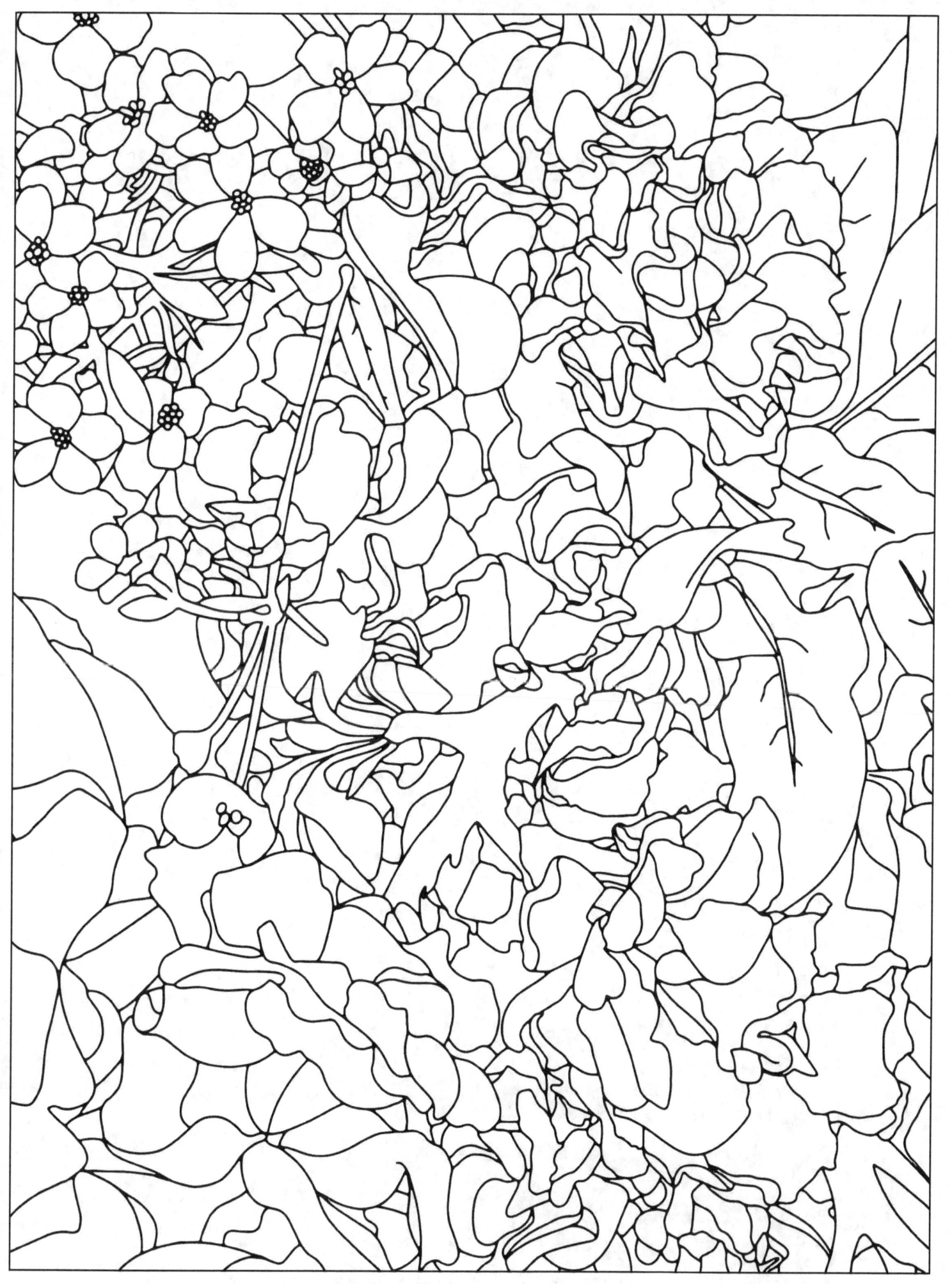

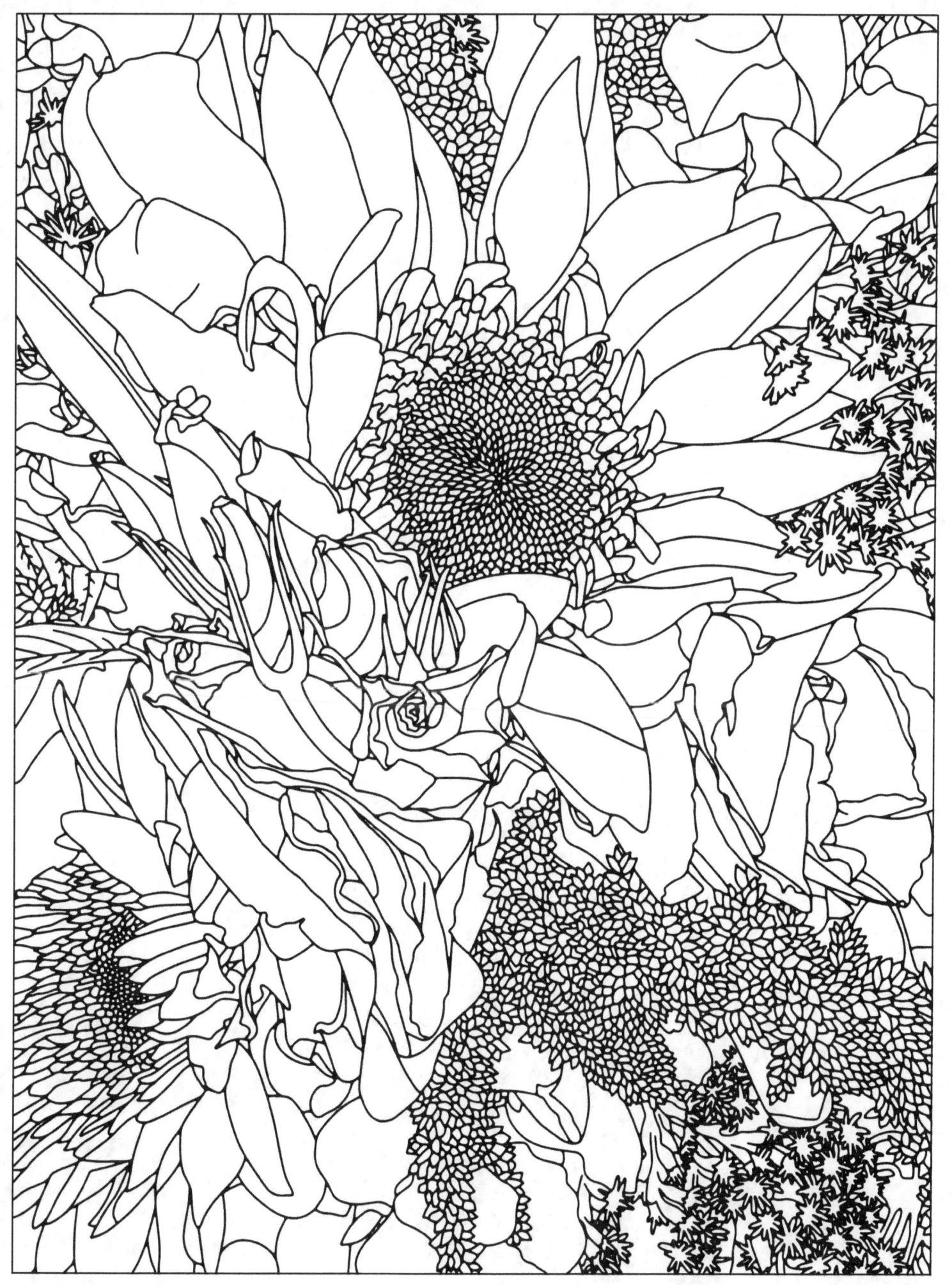

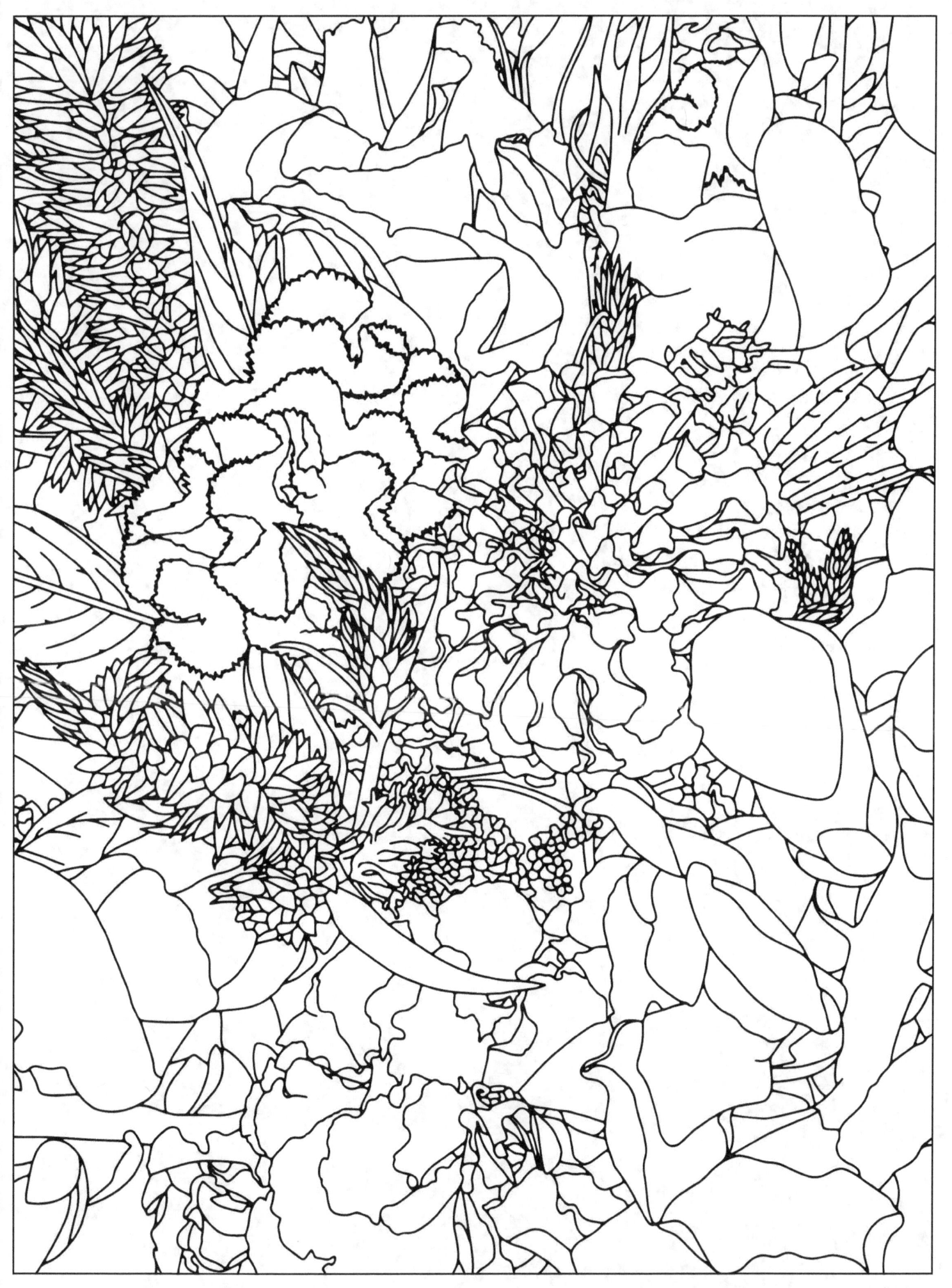

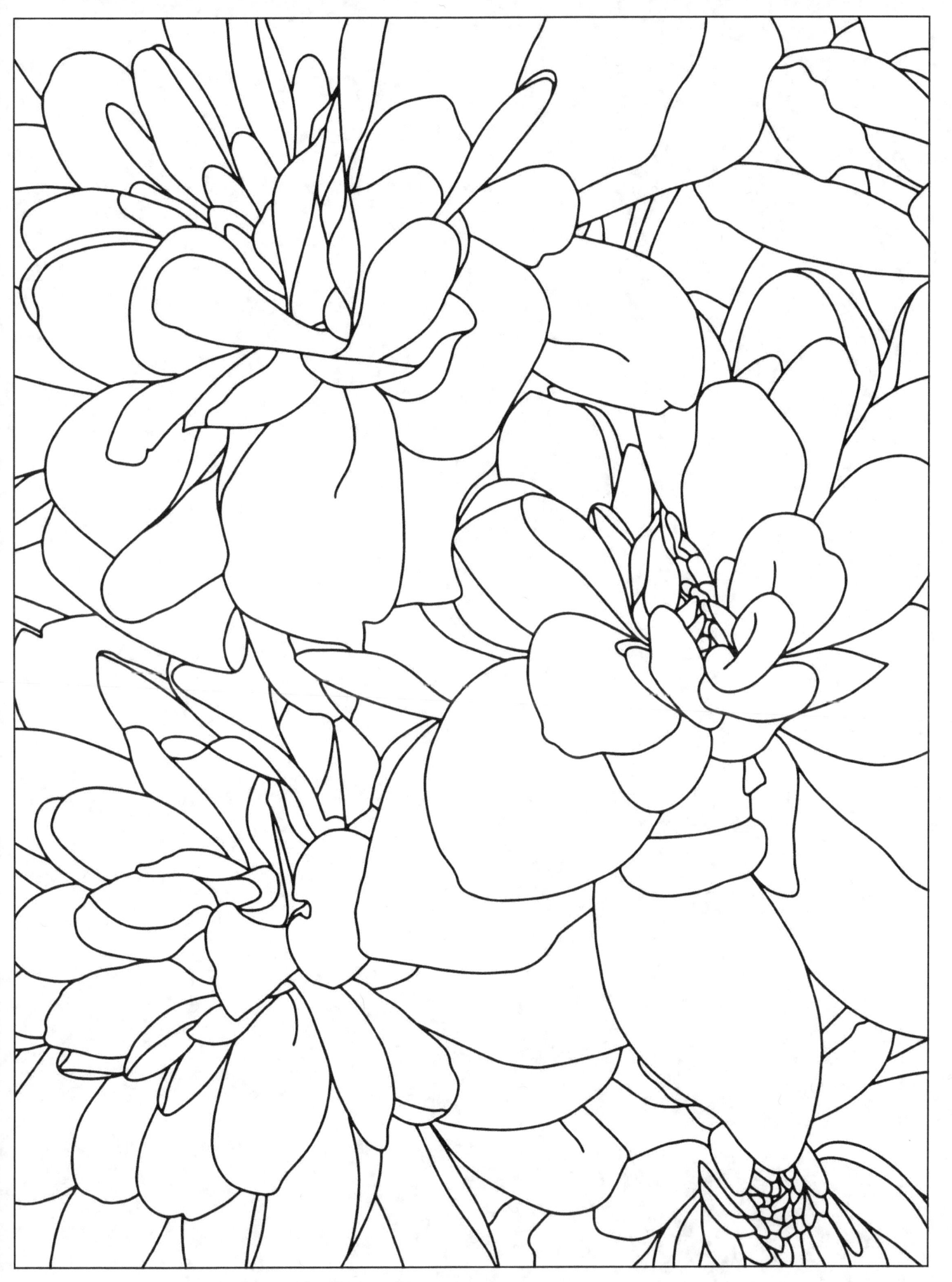

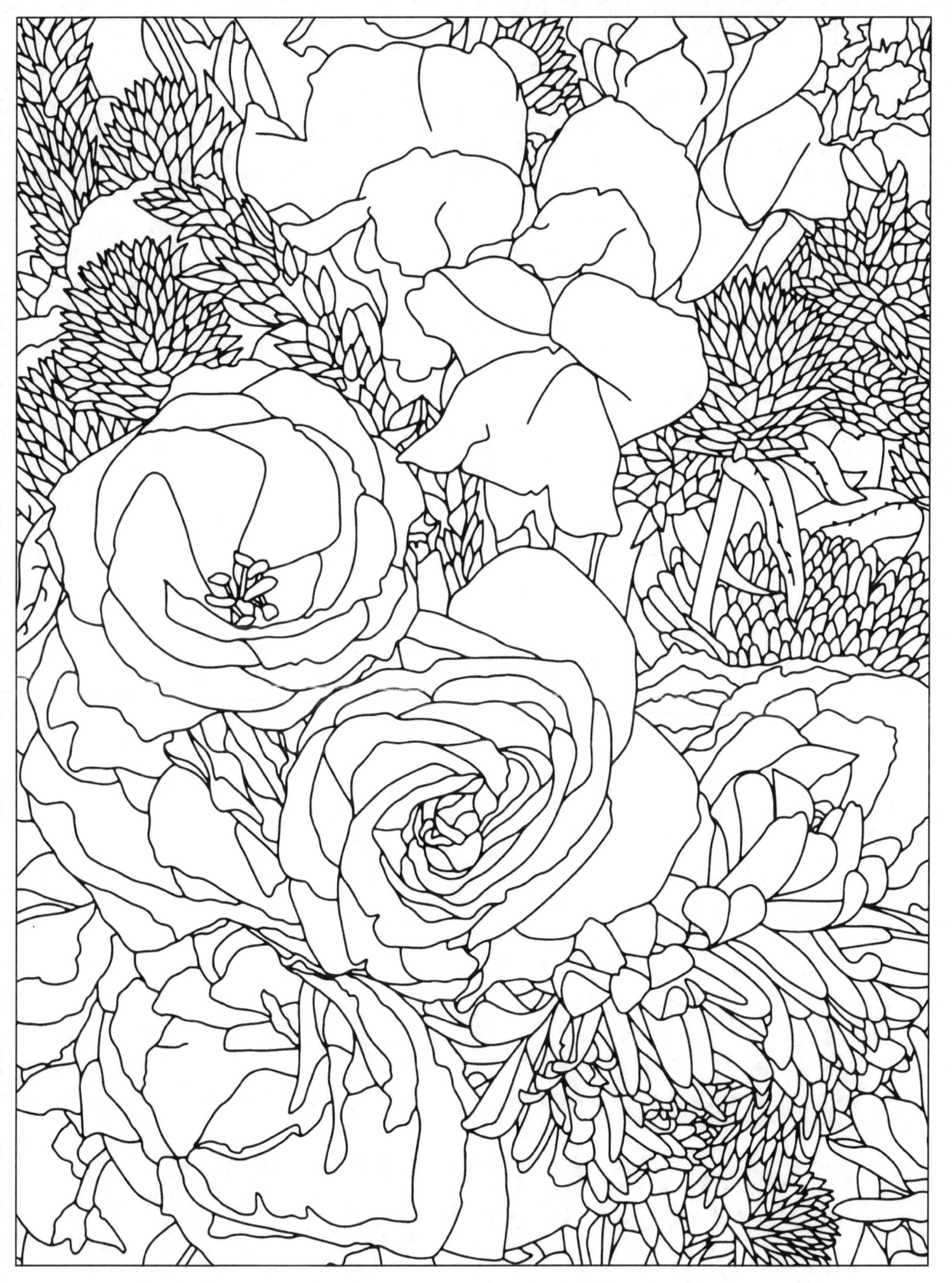

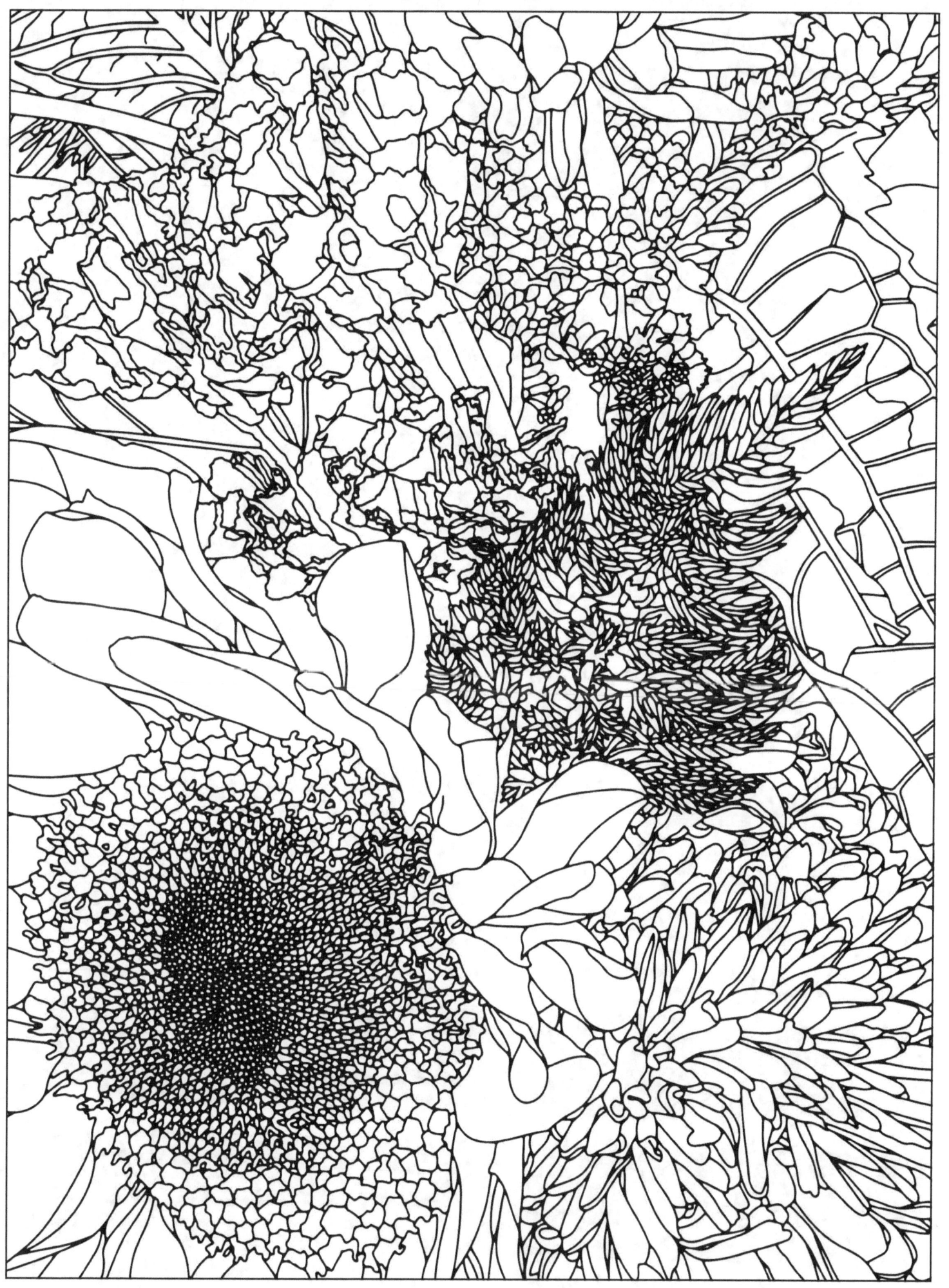

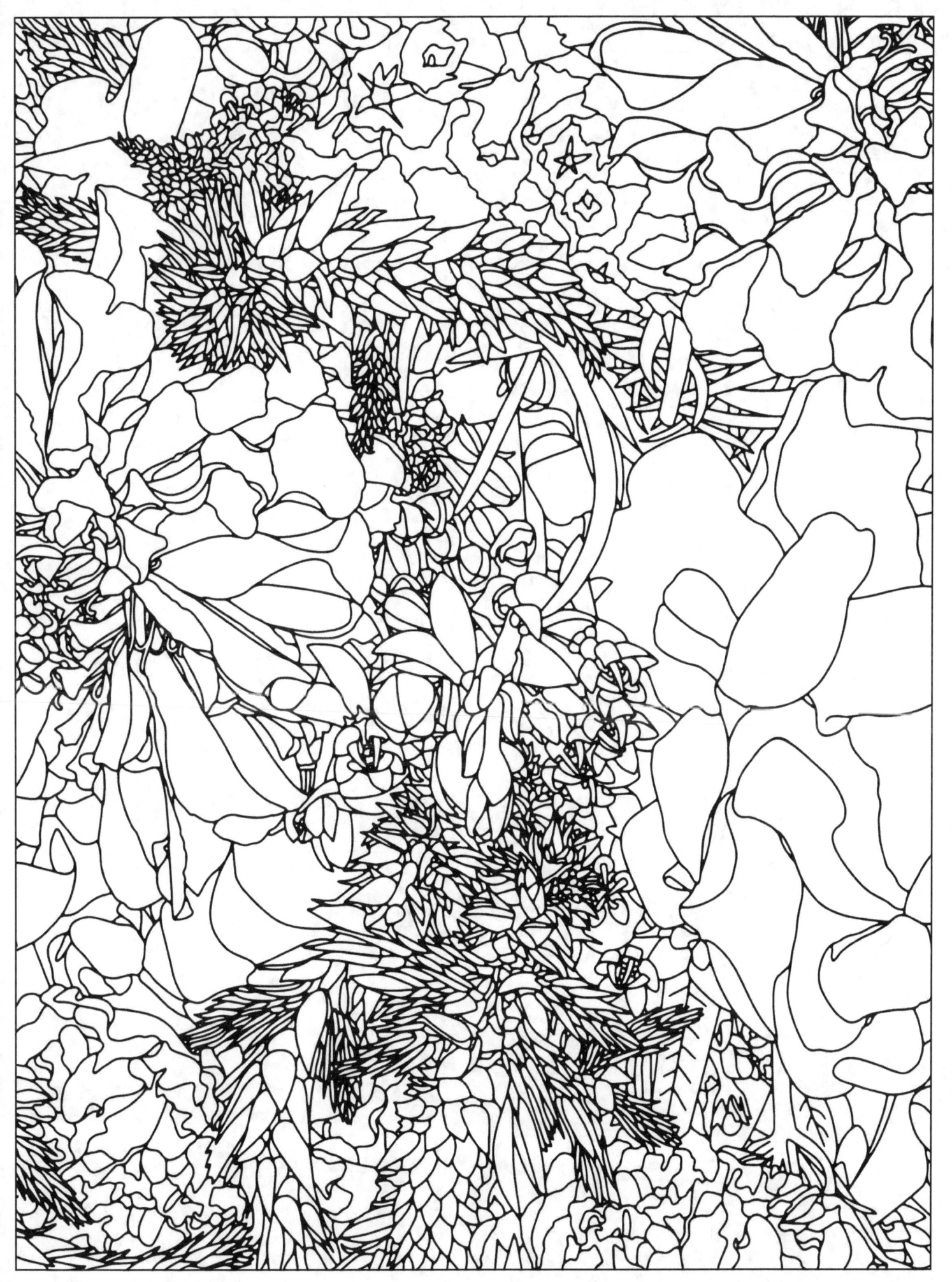

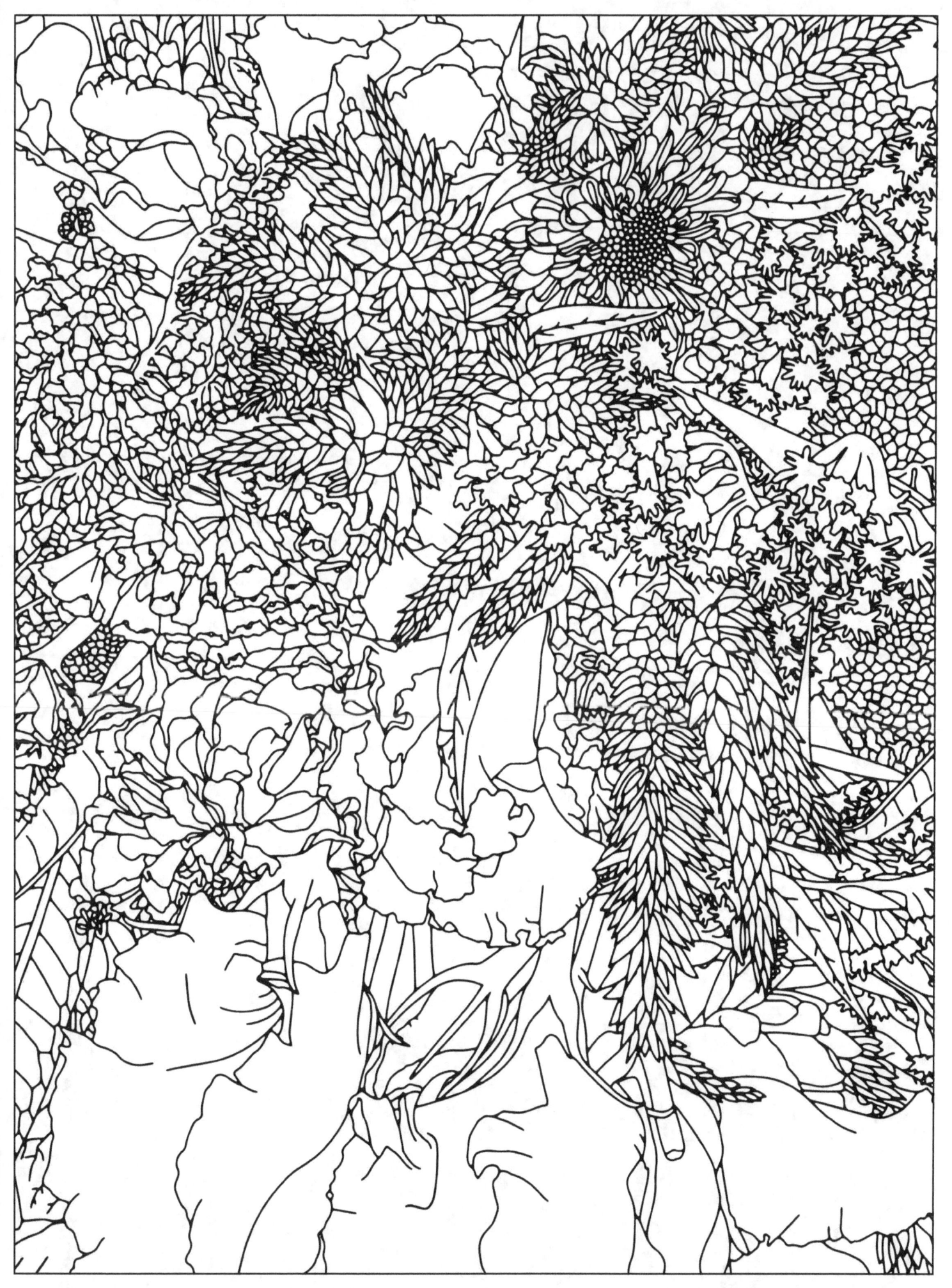

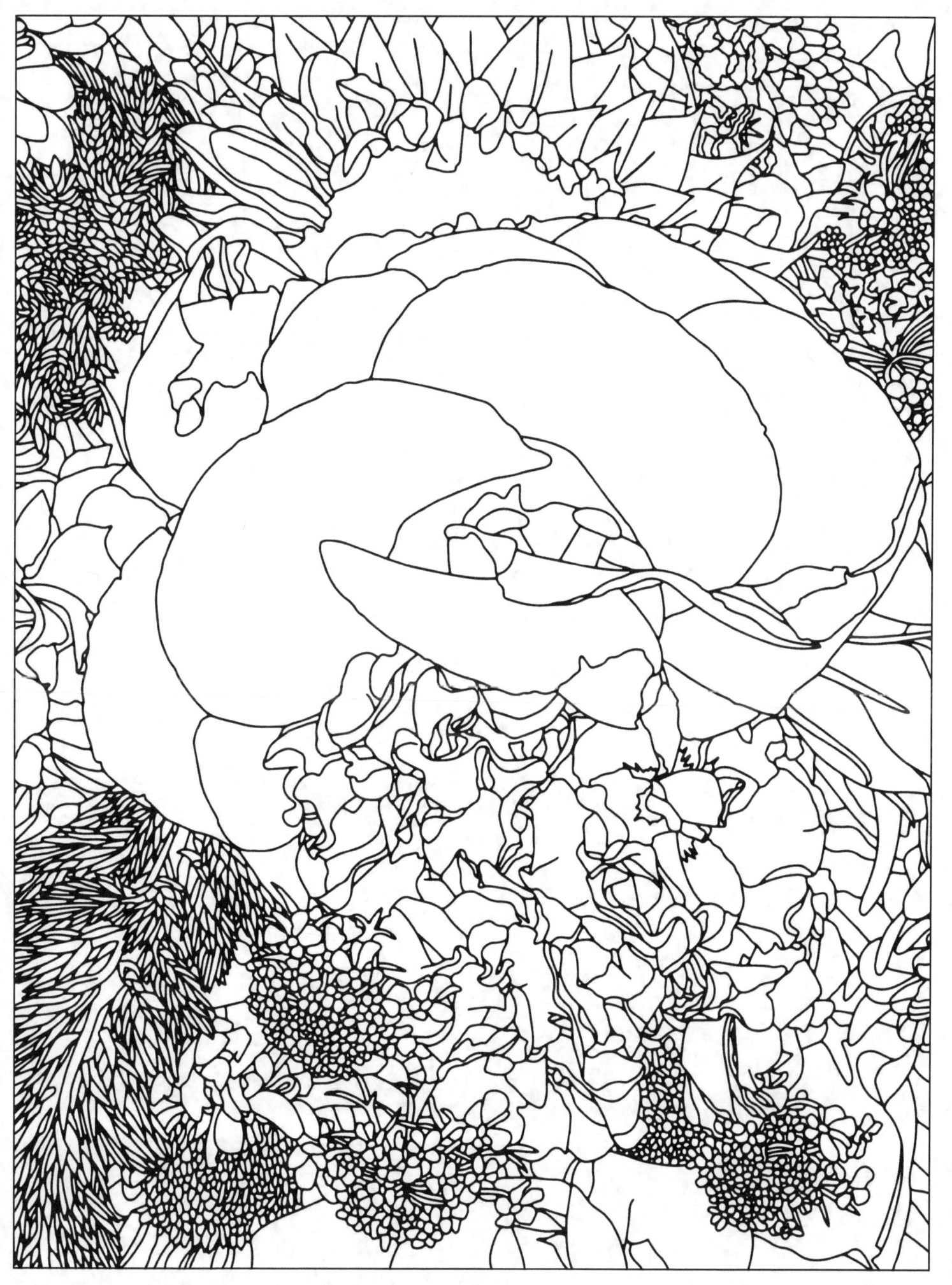

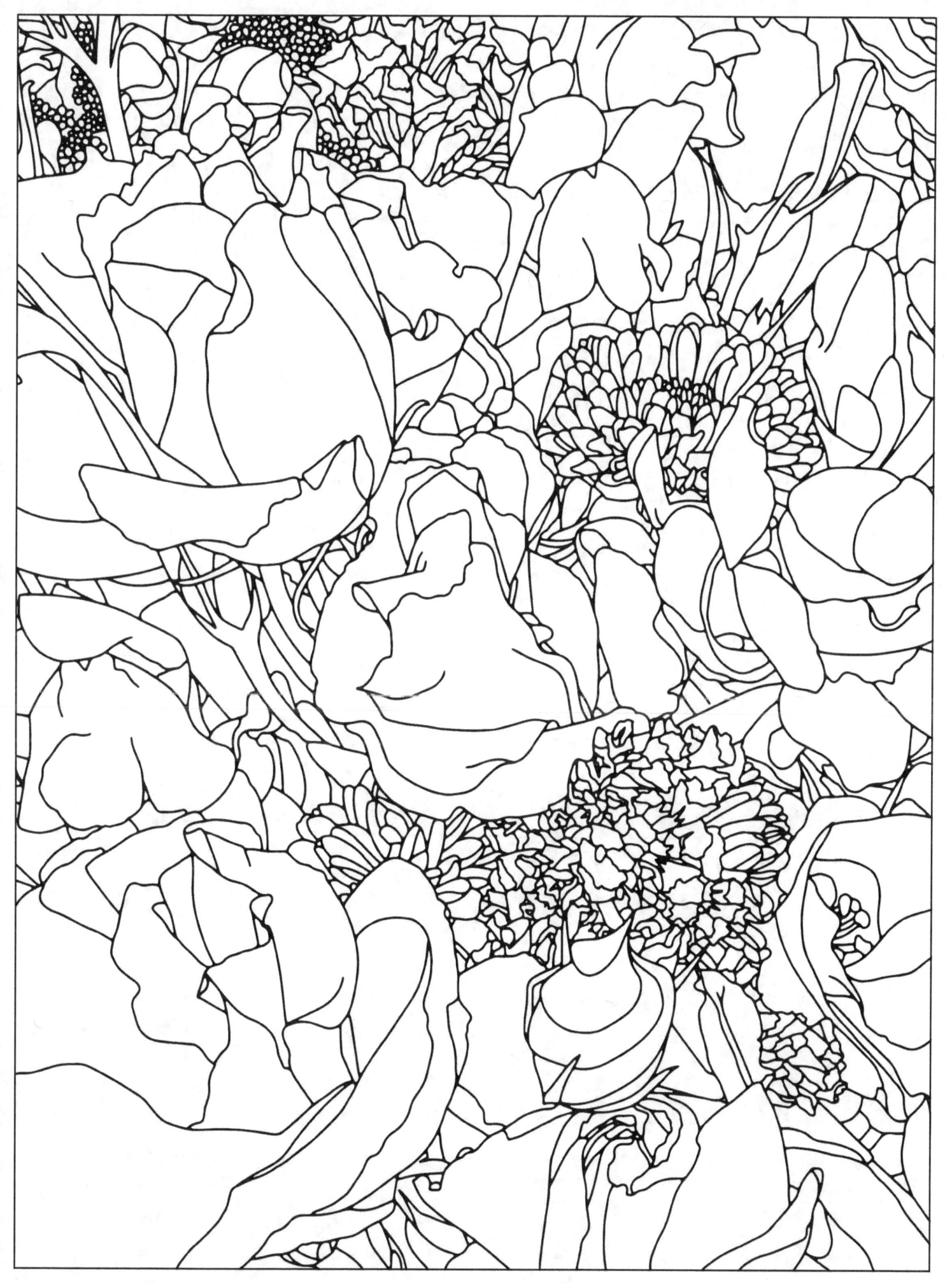

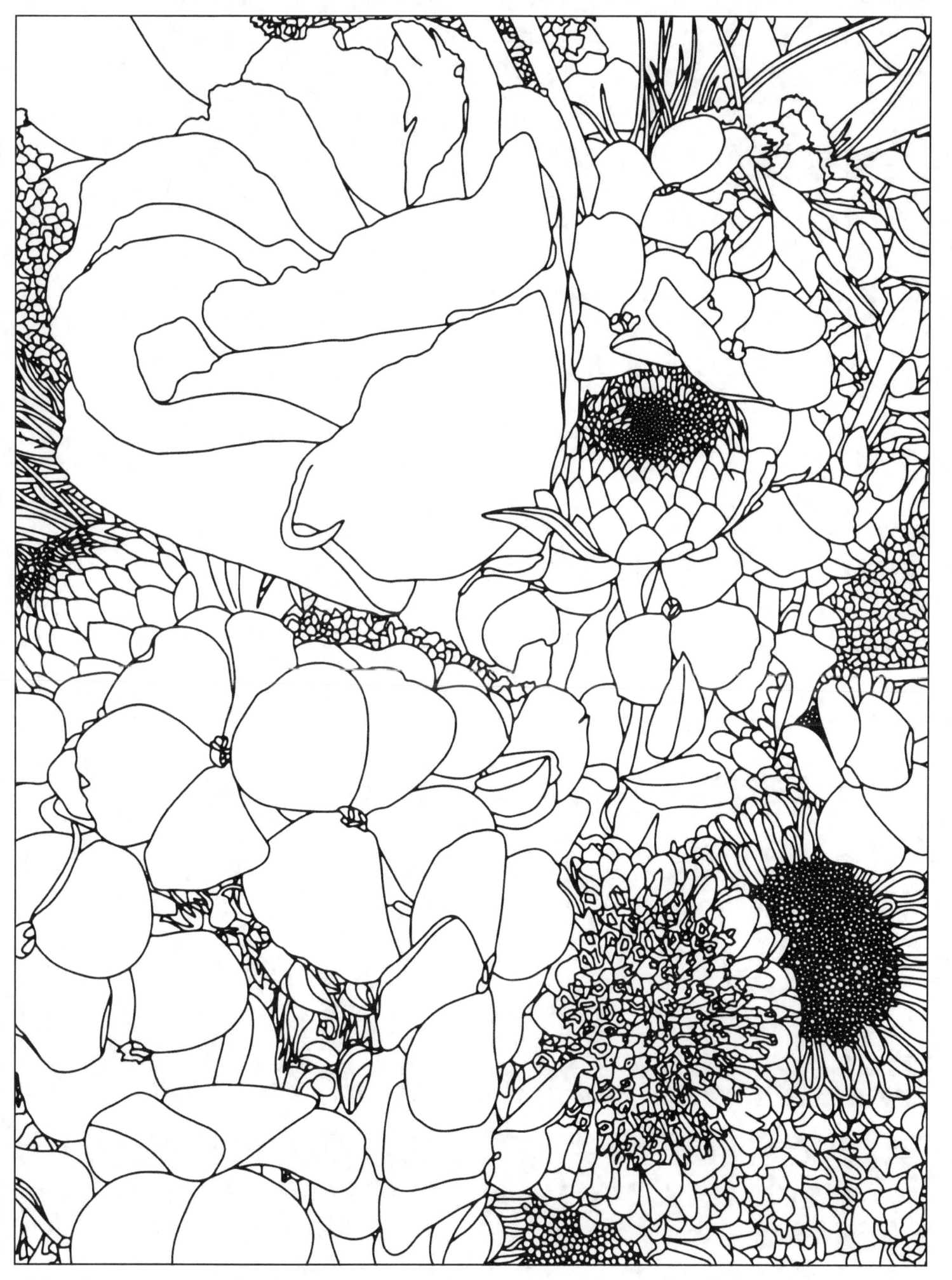

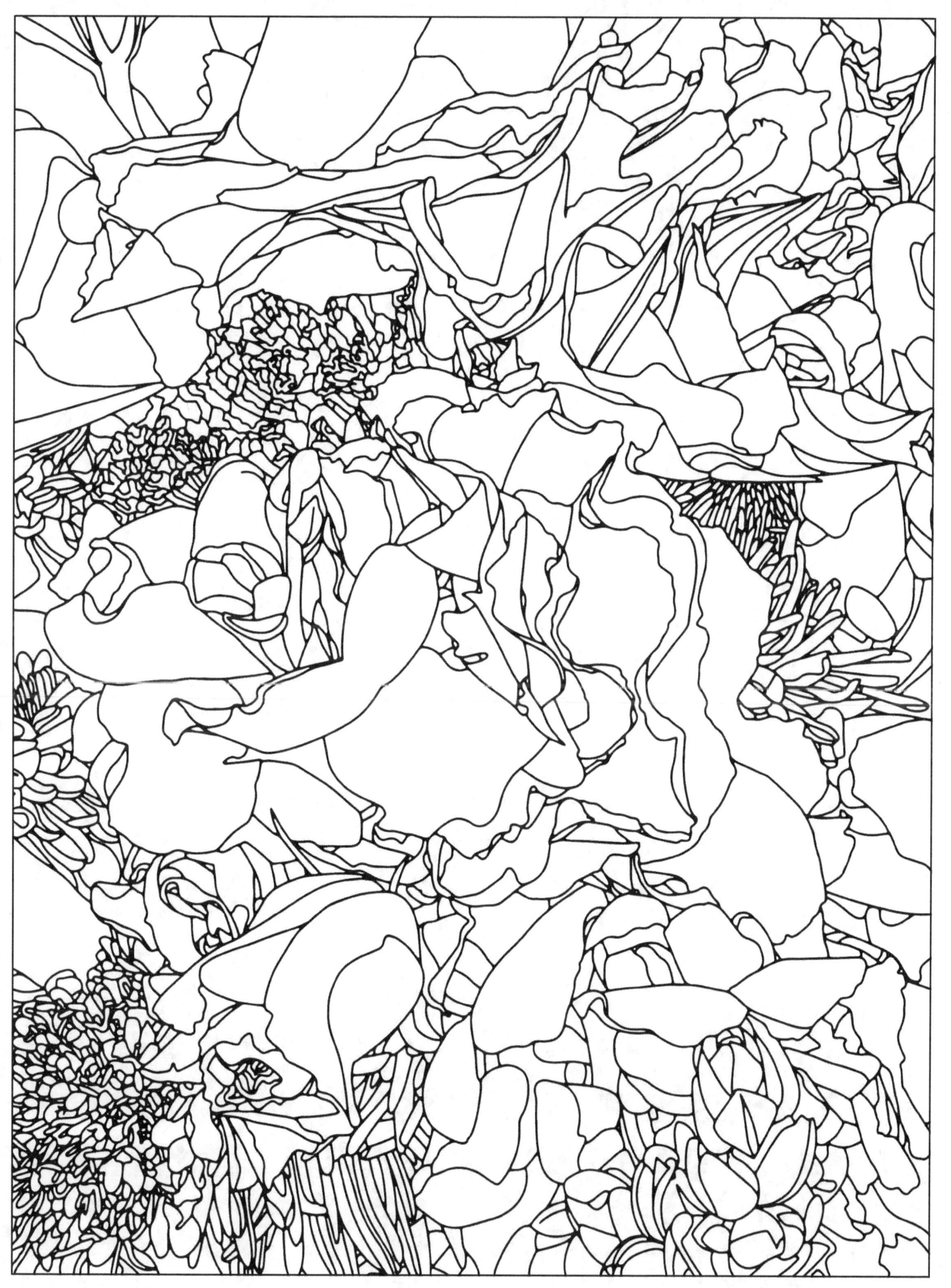

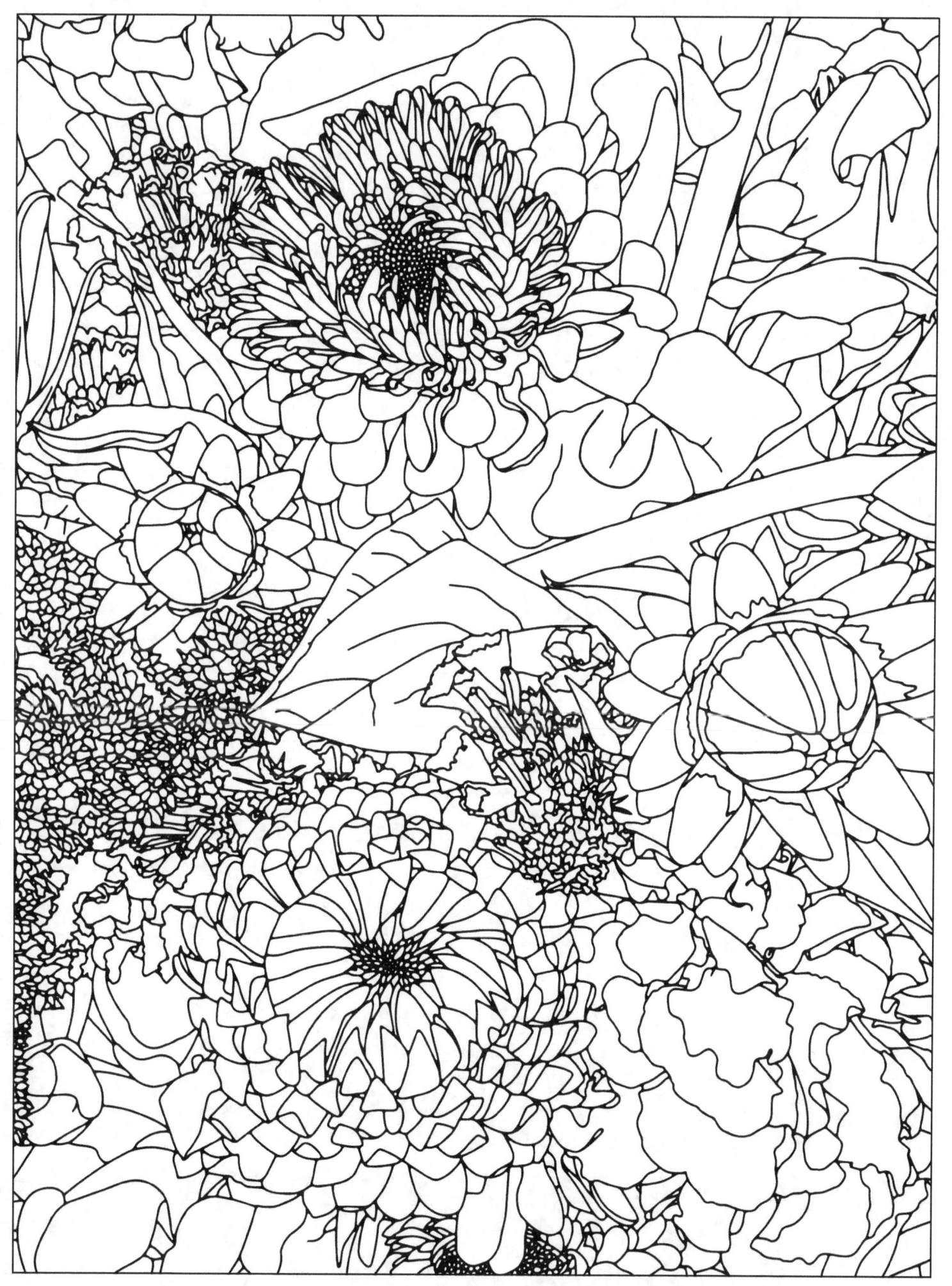

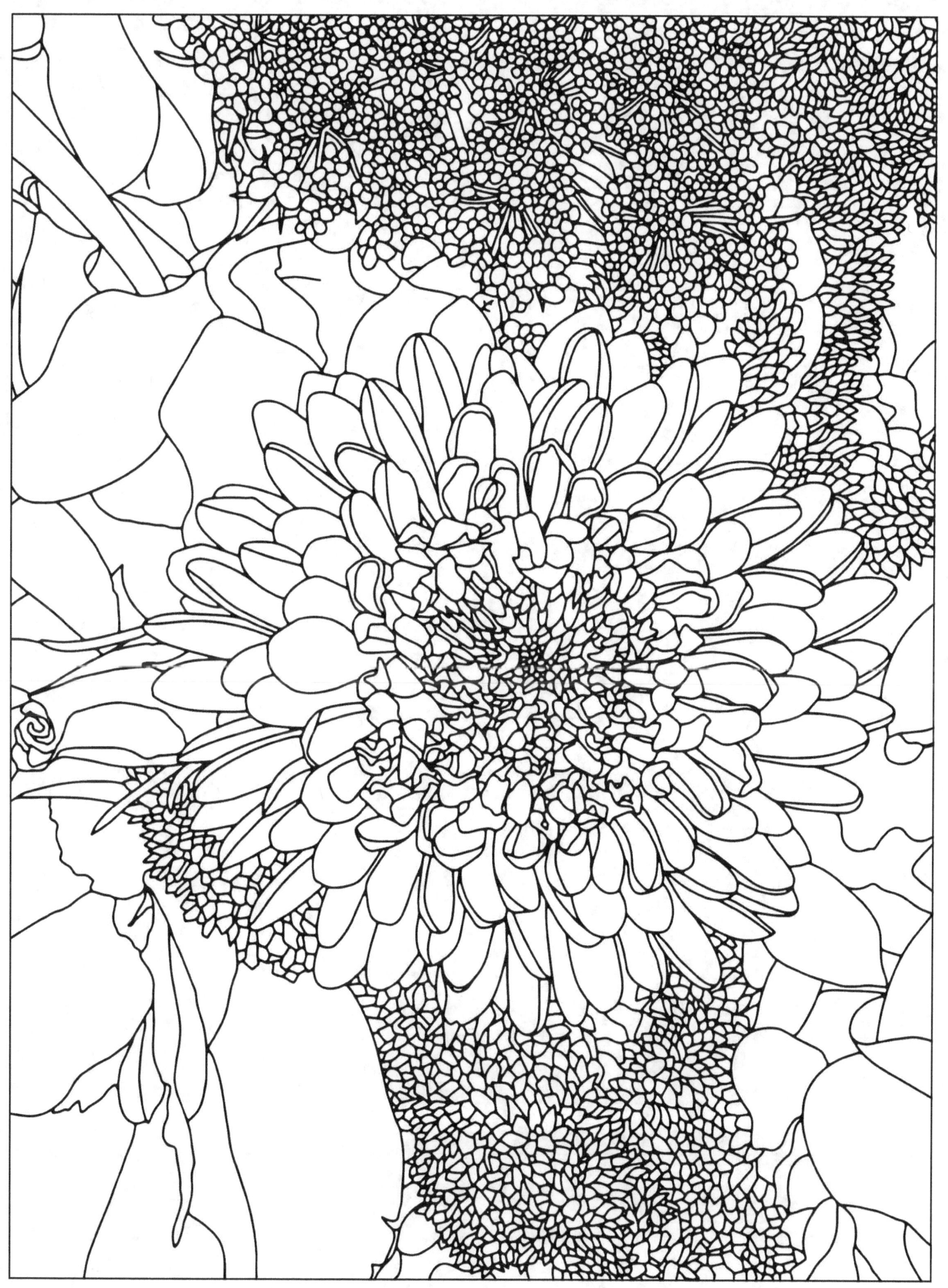

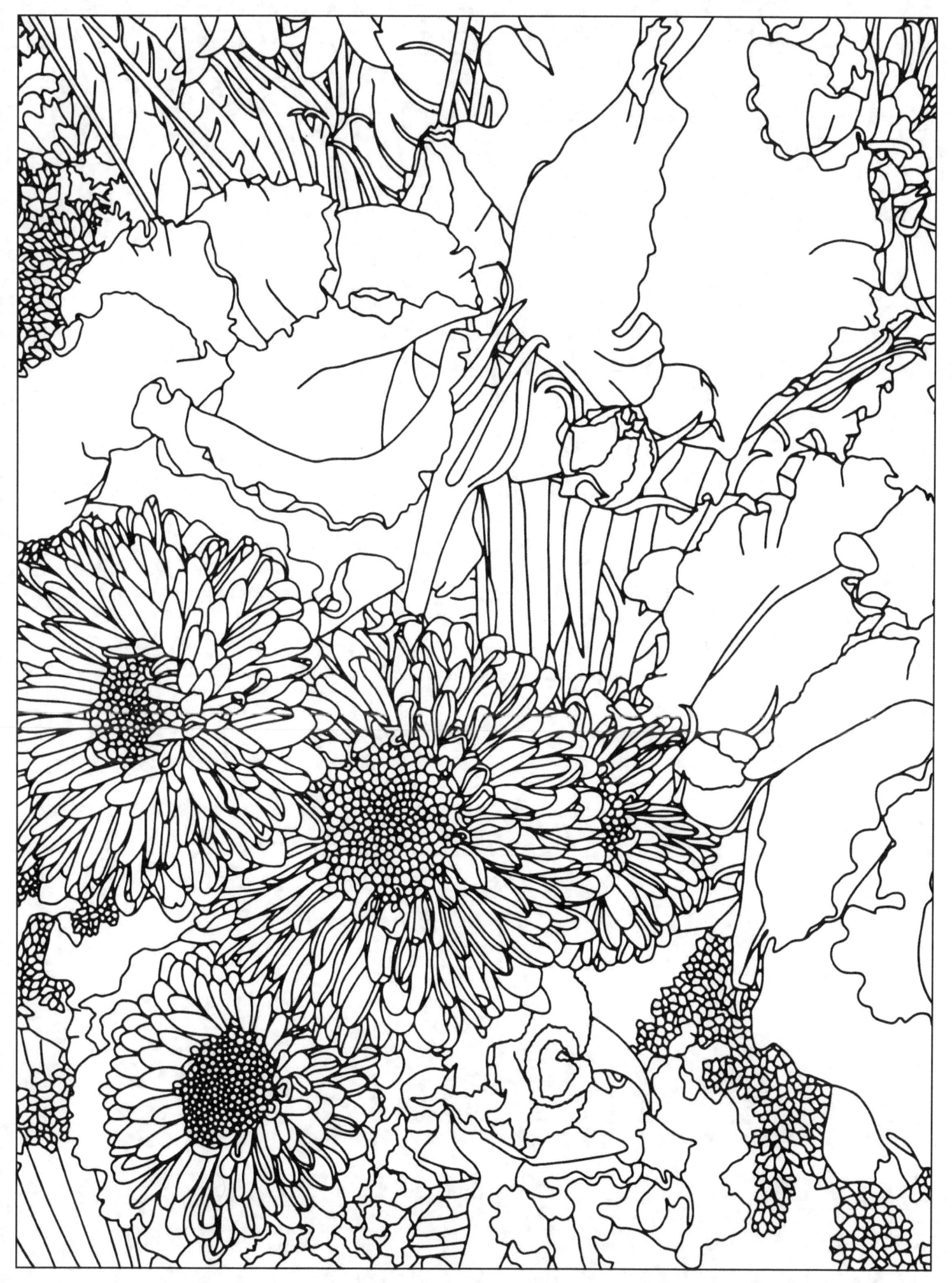

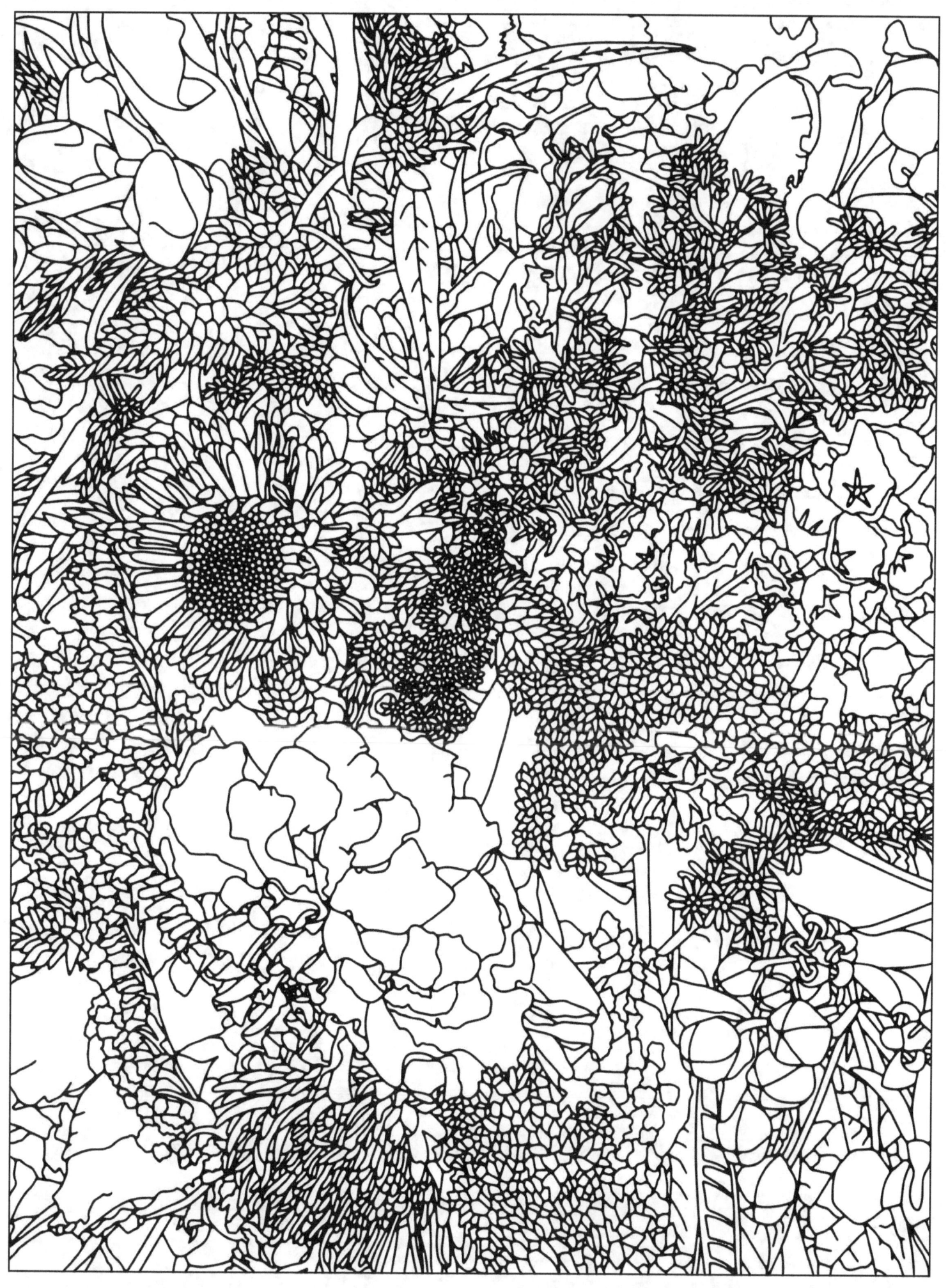

Test out your colors here!

Doodle and see how your colors work for this book!

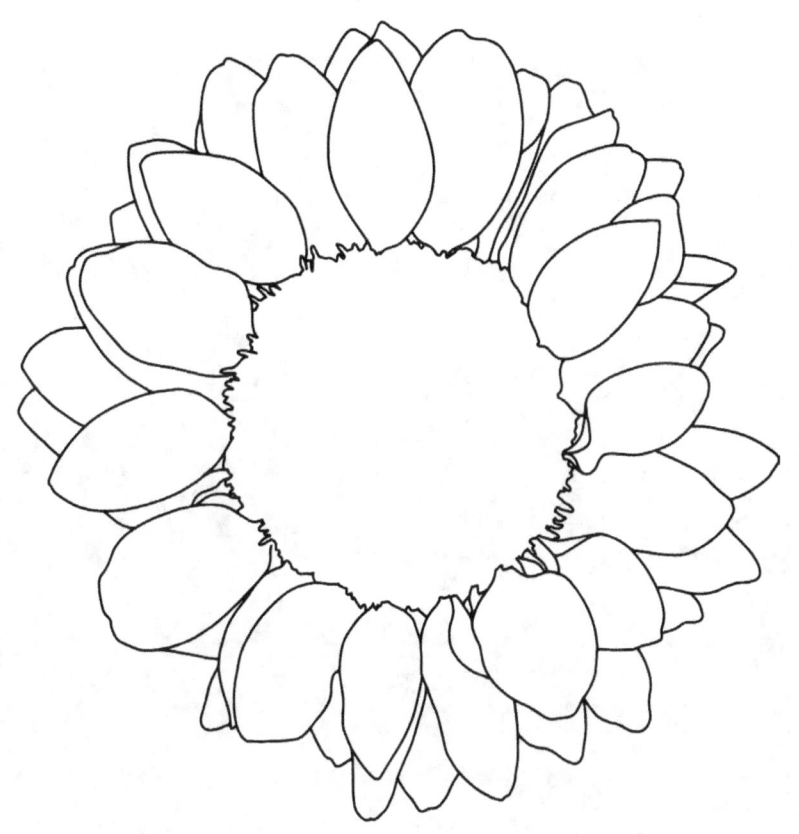

Extra Page

This page can be removed to place behind the page you're coloring to ensure there is no bleed through from your markers!

P.S.- You're wonderful, and never let anyone tell you any different!

www.ingramcontent.com/pod-product-compliance
Lightning Source LLC
Chambersburg PA
CBHW081123240526
45470CB00019B/2923

Mandy Kay's Coloring for Days

Sweet Treats Edition

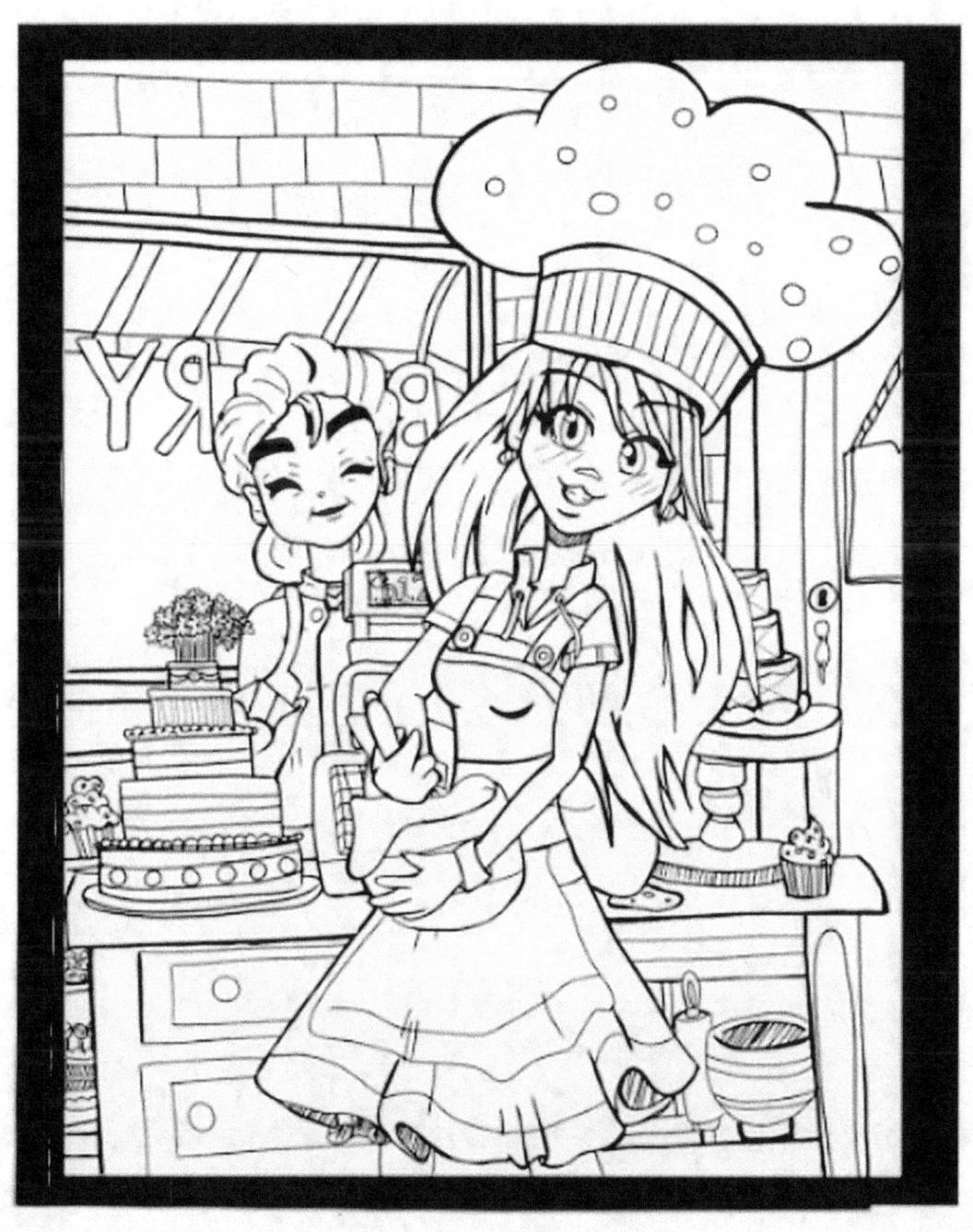

Art by Amanda Kern